101 ELEPHANT JOKES

Compiled by ROBERT BLAKE

Illustrated by William Hogarth

SCHOLASTIC BOOK SERVICES
NEW YORK•TORONTO•LONDON•AUCKLAND•SYDNEY•TOKYO

Dedicated to Miss Kathryn Sapios,
my math teacher who gave much of
her time and advice to help me
prepare this book, and to all those
who contributed and suggested.

ISBN: 0-590-08078-4

31 30 29 28 27 26 25   9/7 0 1 2 3 4/8
                Printed in the U.S.A.

Dear friends of elephants:

One noon hour not long ago a secretary put her head in my door and said: "There's a boy at the reception desk. He wants to talk to an editor."

The boy came in and untied a sheaf of folded brown wrapping paper. "This," he said, "is what teenagers want. I know because I'm a member of the Teenage Book Club."

The hand-lettered top page read *101 Elephant Jokes* by Bob Blake. "Elephant jokes have had their day," I said. "Everybody knows them or will soon. Are these *new* elephant jokes?"

"You don't understand," said young Mr. Blake. "Newness isn't important. The important thing to a teenager is this: if somebody says, 'Why does an elephant do'—well, anything . . . . *you've* got to know the answer. That's why I've collected all the *best* elephant jokes. There are also some new ones my friends and I made up."

"Let's see if they make me laugh," I said.

They did. I showed the 101 jokes to other editors. They laughed. The editors and Bob Blake hope you will too.

Bob Blake is 14—our youngest Scholastic Book Services author. He attends the Memorial Junior High School, Fair Lawn, N. J., where he edits the school newspaper.

"Why are elephants' tusks easier to get in Alabama?"

Well, that proves it. Maybe *you* don't know all 101 elephant jokes!

Yours for laughter,

William Dow Boutwell
Editorial Vice President

Warning:
Practically no parents will think elephant jokes are funny.

If an elephant didn't have a trunk, how would he smell?

Trunk or no trunk, he'd still smell terrible.

What's red, blue, yellow, green, orange, purple, and white?

A Madras elephant.

How do you kill a Madras elephant?

Put him in a tub of water and let him bleed.

How do you kill a blue elephant?

With a blue shotgun.

Why do elephants have wrinkled knees?

From playing marbles.

How do you kill a pink elephant?

Twist his trunk until it turns blue and kill him with a blue shotgun.

Why do elephants have sore ankles?

From wearing their sneakers too tight!

Why do ducks have webbed feet?

To stamp out forest fires!

Why do elephants have flat feet?

To stamp out burning ducks!

Why can't an elephant ride a bicycle?

He doesn't have a thumb to ring the bell.

Why do elephants wear blue sneakers?

Their red ones are in the laundry!

Why do elephants wear green sneakers?

To hide in the grass!

What's the difference between a plum and an elephant?

Their color!

What did one elephant say to the other?

Nothing! Elephants can't talk!

How do you stop a herd of elephants from charging?

Take away their credit cards!

What did Tarzan say when he saw the elephants coming?

"Here come the elephants!"

What did Jane say?

"Here come the plums!" (She was colorblind!!)

Why does an elephant lie on his back?

To trip low-flying canaries!

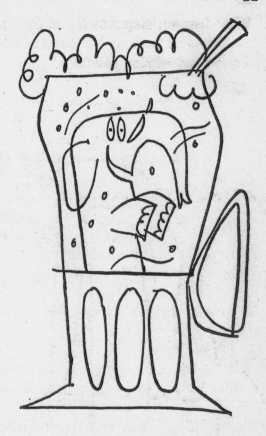

How do you make an elephant float?

Two scoops of ice cream, soda, and some elephant!

What do you know when you see three elephants walking down the street wearing pink sweatshirts?

They're all on the same team!

How do you get down from an elephant?

You don't! You get down from a duck!

Why don't many elephants go to college?

Because they don't finish high school!

What's red and white on the outside and gray and white on the inside?

Campbell's Cream of Elephant Soup!

Why do elephants have squinting eyes?

*From reading the small print on peanut
    packages!*

Why does an elephant have a short tail?

Someone pulled his trunk!

Why do elephants have flat feet?

*They don't have arches in their sneak-
    ers!*

What did Tarzan say when he saw the
    elephants coming down the path
    wearing sunglasses?

Nothing! He couldn't recognize them!

Why did the elephant fall out of a palm
tree?

A hippopotamus pushed him out!

What's the similarity between a plum
and an elephant?

*They're both purple, except for the
elephant!*

How can you tell when there's an elephant in your refrigerator?

*You can see his footprints in the cheese-
cake!*

Why do elephants have round feet?

To walk on the lily pads!

What did Charles de Gaulle say when
he saw the elephants coming down
the path?

Voilá les éléphants down the path!

What did the elephants say when they saw de Gaulle?

Nothing! Elephants can't speak French!

Why do girl elephants wear angora sweaters?

To tell them apart from boy elephants!

What has twelve legs, is pink, and goes "Bah, Bah, Bah"?

Three pink elephants singing the "Whiffenpoof Song!"

Why do elephants climb up palm trees?

To try out their new sneakers!

How do you fit six elephants in your car?

Three in the back; three in the front!

How do you fit six elephants in a Volks-
wagon?

*Three in the back; two in the front; and
one in the glove compartment!*

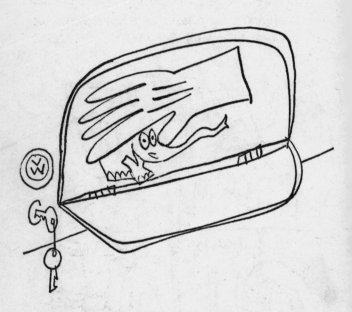

One way to catch elephants:

*Hide in the grass and make a noise
like a peanut!*

Still another way to catch elephants:

Make a sign spelling elephants wrong: "Elefunts." Elephants will come along, see the sign, and begin to laugh. Take a pair of binoculars and look through the wrong end. Pick the elephants up with tweezers and drop them in a milk bottle!

Why do elephants wear glasses?

To make sure they don't step on other elephants!

How do you get an elephant out of a box of Jello?

Follow the directions on the back of the package!

Why did the elephant lie on his back in the water and stick his feet up?

So you could tell him from a bar of Ivory soap!

Why did the eleph marry the ant?

He wanted to have Eleph-ants!

Why do elephants hide behind trees?

To trip ants!

Why do elephants wear green caps?

So they can tip-toe across a pool table without being seen!

Why do elephants have gray skin?

From "iron-poor blood!"

How does an elephant get in a tree?

He hides in an acorn and waits for a squirrel to carry him up!

How does an elephant get down from a tree?

He sits on a leaf and waits for the wind to carry him down!

Why does an elephant climb a tree?

To get in his nest!

Why did the elephant and the donkey
fight?

It was an election year!

Why do elephants catch colds?

*You would too if you ran around with-
out any clothes on!*

Why do elephants have short tails?

So they won't get them caught in sub-way doors!

Why do elephants have white tusks?

They use the Crest formula!

Why do elephants' tusks stick 'way out?

Because their parents won't allow them to get braces!

Why do elephants live in jungles?

It's away from the high-rent district!

Why do elephants have long toenails on
Friday?

*Because their manicurist doesn't come
until Saturday!*

Why do elephants wear sneakers while jumping from tree to tree?

They don't want to wake up the neigh-bors!

How do you lift an elephant?

Put him on an acorn and wait twenty years!

Are you sick yet? If not, you will be by the time you reach the end! If you don't think you survive reading another one of these jokes, you had better burn this book give it to an enemy. (You don't want a friend to get sick, do you?)

So you think you'll live through it? Well, just wait. You'll be tickled to DEATH!

What's gray and white and red all over?

An embarrassed elephant!

④

⑤ inside out!

What do elephants have that no other animal has?

Baby elephants!

What's gray and lights up?

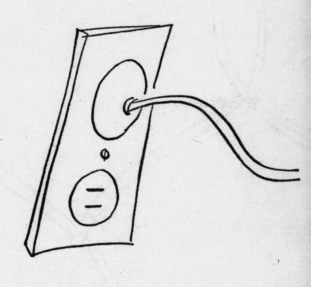

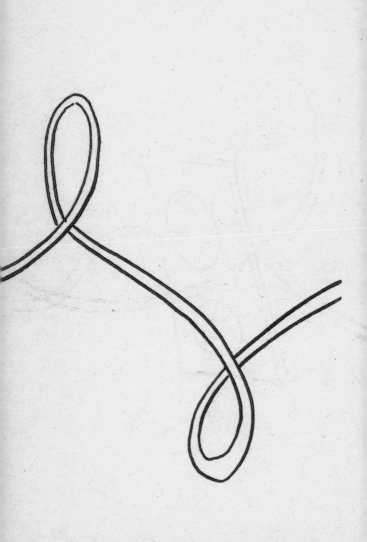

An electric elephant!

How do elephants earn extra money?

They baby-sit for bluebirds on Saturday nights!

Why don't elephants laugh?

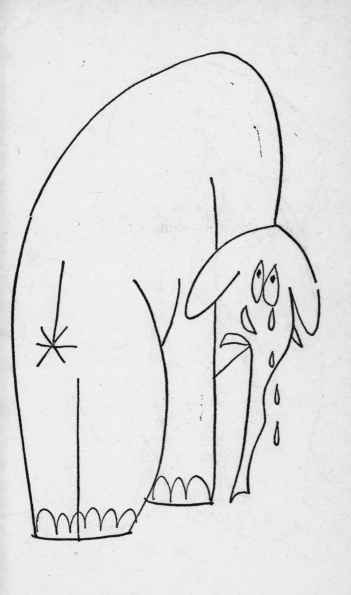

*With all these sickening elephant jokes
going around, how can they?!*

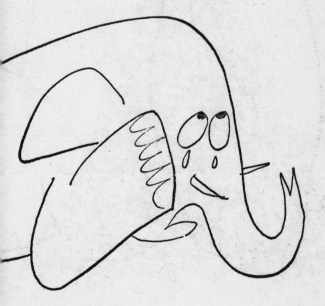

Why do elephants like peanuts?

Because they can save the peanut wrappers for valuable prizes!

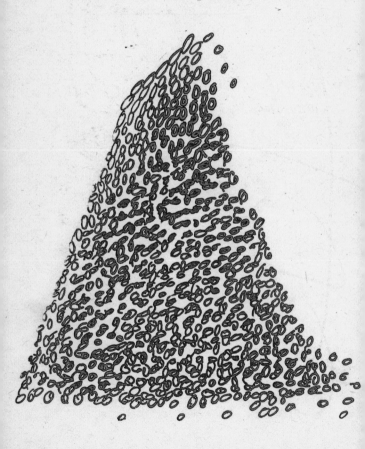

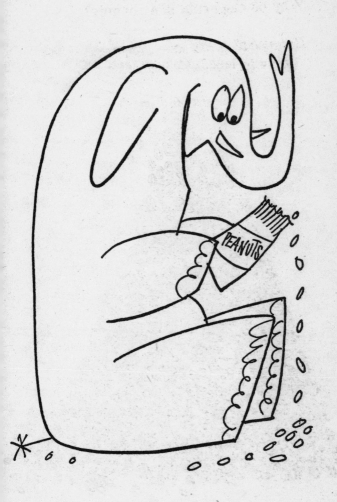

Why do elephants have teeth?

To chew their toenails!

Why do elephants have toenails?

So they can have something to chew!

Why do elephants have trunks?

They can't afford suitcases!

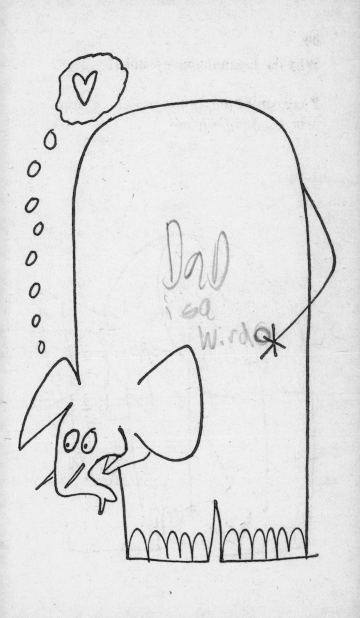

Why do elephants wear short-shorts?

You'd sweat too, if you wore long pants in the jungle heat!

What's the difference between ? girl
elephant and a boy elephant?

One sings soprano, one sings bass!

How do elephants dive into swimming pools?

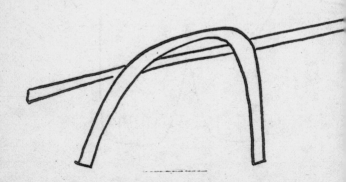

Head first!

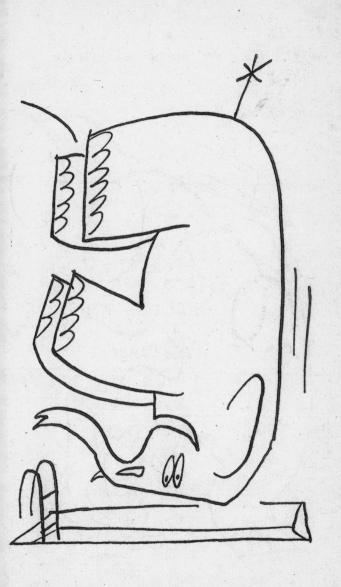

What's gray and stamps out jungle fires?

Smokey, the Elephant!

What's Smokey the Elephant's middle name?

THE!

How do you run over an elephant?

Climb up his tail, dash to his head, then slide down the trunk!!

Why do elephants go to bed late?

They spend hours setting their tails!

Why are elephants gray?

So you can tell them from bluebirds!

Why do elephants step on the lily pads?

The water won't hold them up!!

Why are elephants trumpeters?

It is too hard for them to learn to play the piano!

How do you make a slow elephant fast?

Don't feed him!

How do you make a statue of an elephant?

Get a stone and carve away all that doesn't look like an elephant!!

Why do elephants have flat feet?

From jumping out of palm trees!

Why is it dangerous to go into the jungle between two and four in the afternoon?

Because that's when elephants are jumping out of trees!

Why are pygmies so small?

They went into the jungle between two and four in the afternoon!

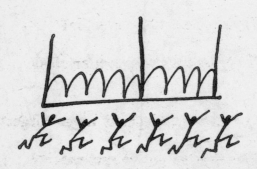

When you buy elephants, what should you always check for first?

The Good Housekeeping "Seal of Approval!"

Why do elephants never lie?

The grass isn't very comfortable!

Why does an elephant never forget?

What has he got to remember?!

Why do elephants drink?

They want to forget!

Why don't elephants listen to the radio?

They don't have fingers to turn the dial!

Where do you find elephants?

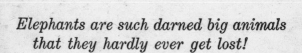

*Elephants are such darned big animals
that they hardly ever get lost!*

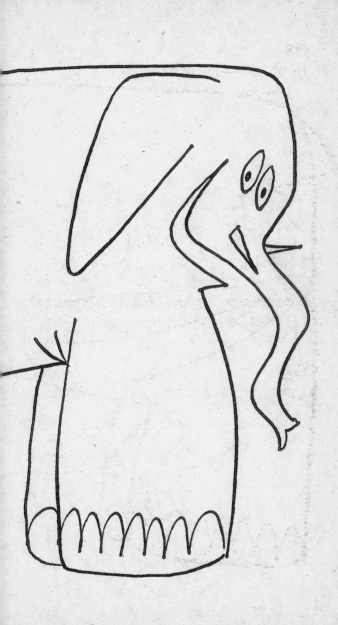

How do you know when there's an elephant in your bathtub?

You can smell the peanuts on his breath!

Why do elephants roll down the hill?

Because they can't roll up very well!

Why do elephants wear sunglasses?

With all this publicity, they are afraid to be recognized!

Why can't elephants hitchhike?

They don't have thumbs!

Why do elephants have dirty knees?

From praying for rain!

What's gray and white and red all over?

A sunburnt elephant!

Why do elephants float down the river
on their backs?

*They don't want to get their tennis shoes
wet!*

Where do you find elephants?

It depends on where you leave them!

What's the difference between an elephant and a flea?

*An elephant can have fleas but a flea
can't have elephants!*

How do elephants get in trees?

They parachute from airplanes!

What do you find between elephants' toes?

Slow running natives!

What color hair tint do elephants use?

How would I know? Only their hair-dressers know for sure!

Why don't elephants take ballet lessons?

They've outgrown their leotards!

Why do elephants have long toenails?

To pick their trunks!

How do you make an elephant stew to serve 1000 guests?

Get a gigantic-sized elephant and cook with potatoes, vegetables, and spices. This is enough to serve 500 people. Throw in two rabbits. Now there's enough to serve 1000 people!!

What weighs two pounds, is gray, and flies?

A two-pound elephant bird!

What time is it when an elephant sits
  on a fence?

Time to buy a new fence!

How can you tell if there's an elephant on your back during a hurricane?

You'll hear his ears flapping in the wind!

Why are elephants' tusks easier to get in Alabama?

Because their "Tuscaloosa."

So! . . . you decided to struggle through to the end, huh? Well, you're not finished! How can you tell whether or not you really know all these jokes? There's only one way: Take the Elephant Quiz!

Be sure to get a good score or you might end up with elephantiasis! So beware!

(Answers at the end)

THE ELEPHANT QUIZ

1. *Why do elephants have wrinkles in their knees?*

   A. From old age!
   B. From playing marbles!
   C. Because they worry too much!

2. *Why do elephants wear glasses?*

   A. To make themselves look glamorous!
   B. So Tarzan won't recognize them!
   C. So they don't step on other elephants!
   D. To cover their baggy eyes!

3. *Why do elephants climb trees?*

   A. To get in their nests!
   B. There's nothing else to climb in the jungle!
   C. Because they think it's lots of fun to do.

4. *Why are elephants gray?*

   A. So you can tell them apart from bluebirds!

   B. Because they'd look pretty funny if they were purple!

   C. Did you ever see one that wasn't gray?

5. *What's red on the outside and gray on the inside?*

   A. An elephant wearing red pajamas!

   B. An elephant swimming in the Red Sea!

   C. Campbell's Cream of Elephant Soup!

6. *Why don't elephants go to college?*

   A. They don't fit through the entrance door!

   B. They don't finish high school!

   C. There are no colleges in the jungle!

 7. *Why don't elephants take ballet lessons?*

   A. They outgrew their leotards!

   B. They learned how to dance in the circus!

   C. They'd rather learn how to play "Monopoly"!

8. *What do you know when you see three elephants walking down the street wearing pink sweatshirts?*

A. It means you've been drinking.
B. You know they're all on the same team.
C. You need a psychiatrist. (Whoever heard of three elephants walking down the street wearing pink sweatshirts?)

9. *What did the elephants say when they saw Charles de Gaulle?*

A. Voilá le Charles de Gaulle!
B. Nothing. . . . Elephants can't speak French!
C. "Say hello to our French relatives"!

10. *Why do elephants wear sneakers while jumping from tree to tree?*

   A. So they won't get their feet dirty!

   B. So they don't get splinters!

   C. So they won't wake up their neighbors!

11. *Why did you buy this ridiculous elephant joke book?*

   A. Because you had 25¢ or 35¢ to waste!

   B. Because you didn't know better!

   C. Because you're sick!

"THE ANSWERS!"

1. - B	6. - B
2. - C	7. - A
3. - A	8. - B
4. - A	9. - B
5. - C	10. - C
	11. - C

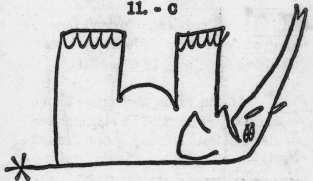

SCORING

 # Right

0   You had better "pack your *trunk*" (!) and catch the next plane out of town before the news gets to the Elephant Kingdom!!

1 to 4   This is the reason your friends are laughing and running the other way.

5 to 7   Watch out! You *still* might end up with "elephantiasis"!

8 to 10   Since elephants don't forget, and you don't either, it looks as though you have something in common!

11!   If you know *that* much about elephants, *you* must *be* an elephant *too* — like me! So . . . come join our Peanut Party!!